Indignation!

Presented

with the compliments of

THE GARDEN
HISTORY SOCIETY

70 Cowcross Street London EC1M 6EJ

www.gardenhistorysociety.org

Indignation!

The campaign for conservation

MAVIS BATEY

DAVID LAMBERT

KIM WILKIE

Kit-Cat

Published in 2000 by
Kit-Cat Books
93 Castelnau
London SW13 9EL

ISBN 0 9538897 0 X

British Library Cataloguing in Publication Data.
A catalogue record of this book is available from the British Library

Designed by Groundwork, Skipton
Typeset in Bitstream Charter
Printed in England by Outset Services Ltd

FRONTISPIECE
The view from Richmond Hill, London.
Indignation at the threat of development led to the first statutory act to save a view.

Contents

ALAN BAXTER

Foreword

Conservation as we think of it today seems to many people to have been a fixed part of our society for some time. But this is not so, and our present position of apparent strength is the result of many hard fought battles over the last four or five generations. Our predecessors' passion and energy have influenced our way of living enormously and for the better. The intellectual and spiritual foundations built by Ruskin and Morris have provided a sure base for the complex construction which now informs our generation's attitude and underpins our planning legislation.

The apparent strength of conservation today is also a danger that leads to complacency. The success in protecting some of the special built heritage has diverted our attention from our low level of care of the great grey areas where many of us live and work. Our human habitat is messy and ugly and degrades the spirit. At the same time, we despoil the wider surroundings as we engulf green fields in tarmac and roar at speed through the countryside. We are now at another crossroads in human history as unbridled technological innovation powers us rapidly into the unknown.

Conservation has to become an all-embracing lifeline that provides the basis for the care of the future and not just the care of the past. Indignation was a powerful human way of responding to threatening new challenges that served well in the past. Can we harness now the energy from a new all-embracing sense of indignation to rework creatively our perception of conservation for the future? To this end the pages that follow are immensely interesting and of real value.

MAVIS BATEY

Introduction

The amenity movement with its campaigns for the sake of both the man-made and the natural environment has evolved through over a century of voluntary grassroots activity. The beginning of the new millennium seems a good time to recall the passionate motivation of those pioneers who fought to save our green and pleasant land and to take heed of what they have to tell us about society, conservation and the environment.

We hope the publication of our book is timely as the Government is currently considering the future development of strategy for the historic environment, 'all those aspects of the country that reflect the shaping hand of human history', and has announced that it intends to undertake a review of conservation policy. If we are considering the future of conservation there is food for thought in remembering how we have arrived where we are in our concern for the environment. We hope that this book will contribute directly to the Government thinking in this important exercise.

Indignation! derives in part from a conference held in Oxford by the Oxford University Department of Continuing Education and the Garden History Society on the eve of Ruskin's centenary to consider his dynamic influence on art, education and environmental conservation. The great moralist had written compellingly in 'The Lamp of Memory',

> God has lent us the earth for our life; it is a great entail. It belongs as much to those who are to come after us, and whose names are already written in the book of creation, as to us; and we have no right, by anything that we do or neglect, to involve them in unnecessary penalties, or deprive them of benefits which it was in our po`wer to bequeath.

These words might have been the opening prayer for the Rio Earth Summit in 1992 when the concept of 'sustainability' was first introduced.

Ruskin and his followers had a holistic approach to the quality of life with an emphasis on good husbandry and environmental stewardship. 'A concern for every one of those things that go to make up the surroundings in which we live'. Ruskin's semi-religious utterances electrified the nineteenth century and his beacon lights or 'lamps', as they became known after his *Seven Lamps of Architecture*, inspired William Morris, Arnold Toynbee, Canon Rawnsley, Octavia Hill and many others to take up passionate 'causes' in pursuit of his aesthetic and social ideals and so lead the way to the voluntary amenity movement.

This grassroots approach to conservation has been the envy of Europe where Napoleonic 'top down' methods have been engrained for so long. There is despair in former communist countries that without our traditions and attitudes it will now be almost impossible to achieve a voluntary amenity movement. In this country conservation legislation has always followed grassroots campaigning and voluntary pilot schemes: listed buildings through the work of the Society for the Protection of Ancient Buildings (SPAB) and the Ancient Monuments Society; open spaces through the Commons and Footpaths Preservation Society (CFPS); country planning, green belts and national parks through the Council for the Preservation of Rural England (CPRE); conservation areas through the Civic Trust and most recently the register of historic parks and gardens following a pilot scheme set up by the Garden History Society.

'Indignation' as the title to this book derives from our notes while we were working together on the Thames Landscape Strategy, a comprehensive survey of the river from Hampton to Kew. The views of local people and interest groups were an important part of the report and we were intrigued to hear from one elderly local historian that in 1901 'indignation meetings' were held on site when the famous view from Richmond Hill was threatened by development. We thought this was a local off the cuff expression until the *Oxford English Dictionary* enlightened us that such protests against public abuses were regularly referred to as 'indignation meetings' and letters to the press as 'indignation letters'.

Indignation seems a fascinating word; it sounds emotional, moral and personal. It is all those things, and the word gives an insight into the nature, and the strength, of the conservation cause. Above all it is personal; the word suggests that the destruction of the view was being taken personally by the good people of Richmond. This is crucial to the matter. Those who went to those indignation meetings felt that they had a personal stake in the landscape which could be shared by fellow members of the community and was above and beyond individual private property rights.

'Indignation' fitted well with Ruskinian moral outrage and the 'causes' taken up by the new societies such as the Commons and Footpaths Preservation Society,

William Morris's SPAB, Octavia Hill's Kyrle Society, the Society for Checking the Abuses of Public Advertising (SCAPA) and the Metropolitan Public Gardens Association which campaigned together with equal fervour for open spaces, ancient buildings, the countryside, clean air, the quality of life, social justice and nature conservation. A good example of how a society started for a specific purpose could extend its ideas to the whole quality of life is provided by SCAPA, set up in 1893 just after the publication of Morris's Utopian *News from Nowhere*. The Secretary of SCAPA, which was later absorbed into the CPRE, is on record as saying, 'our mission is, in one aspect, to save civilization, and, in another, to mitigate a nuisance. In pursuit of one ideal we are advancing the other'.

Ruskin's guiding 'lamp of beauty' was still the ideal and, as the wife of SCAPA's president urged, there was a bounden need to educate and 'help others to see and understand this beautiful world as well'. The movement which gathered strength at the end of the century substituted the more politically manageable word 'amenity' for that of 'beauty' when it called for the government to set up a parliamentary amenity committee and a Minister of Amenities. The word was already in current use with an environmental association; the eighteenth century had made much of the idealised *locus amoenus* of classical mythology and through landscape gardening had fostered a visual appreciation of sur-roundings and what constituted 'amoenities'. Today the emphasis of the word is unfortunately on convenience, as in the municipal amenity tip, a far cry from the original Elysian 'pleasant place'.

Amenity was first used as a planning concept in the 1909 Housing and Town Planning Act when responsibility for safeguarding the 'amenity of the area' was vested in local government. This seemed a step in the right direction, but it soon became apparent that 'causes' would not be greatly advanced unless the citizens were prepared to agitate and remind local authorities of their powers and opportunities. With this in mind local amenity societies then began to be set up all over the country, giving a new importance to the role of the local community in conservation. A major part of the indignation of the amenity movement that followed stemmed from frustration at the half-hearted applica-tion of the local by-laws that had been conceded and an inability to get any form of statutory control for its concerns. All efforts on the Government's part in this direction had to be suspended at the outbreak of war in 1914.

The determined action by the new national amenity societies set up after the end of the war in the twenties and thirties, including the Ancient Monuments

Society, the CPRE and the Georgian Group, was given a boost by spirited contributions from eminent people in Clough Williams-Ellis's book, *Britain and the Beast*, exposing the iniquitous effect of *laissez-faire* on the environment. Clough Williams-Ellis said in his introduction, 'We are at the beginning of our lease, not the end of it – a long lease from Nature, who, though a kindly landlord enough, is slow to repair the damage done by her vandal tenants'. These words harked back to the creed of Ruskin and Morris on the need for environmental stewardship.

Town and country planning was seen as essential to curb the 'Beast' of despoliation. It is good to find that this was not to be a political issue. When the CPRE was founded in 1926, the leaders of the three political parties, Stanley Baldwin, Ramsay Macdonald and Lloyd George wrote a combined letter of congratulations to *The Times*. In a parliamentary debate in the 1930s it was said by Josiah Wedgwood, 'The Labour party are not usually considered conservative, but we are conservative when it is a case of preserving the natural beauty of England… in this case Socialism and Conservatism are bound together'. Interestingly enough, Ruskin, in spite of his influence on radical thinking, was a conservative and Morris a socialist.

Unfortunately any progress towards protecting the built and natural environment was once again brought to an abrupt halt in 1939. A determined effort was made at the end of the war to salvage what remained of Britain's heritage with the setting up of a Ministry of Town and Country Planning as a central authority. Excellent news as this was for conservation and the introduction of the listing of buildings, by 1954 John Harvey, who had been a pioneer in the listing process and was a dedicated conservationist and effective supporter of many amenity societies, warned that there was a danger of complacency setting in; he stressed the problems of bureaucracy which statutory protection of necessity brought with it and the gulf that lay between theory and practice in preservation. His 'national sense of indignation' had still a vital role to play.

It is nearly fifty years since John Harvey uttered these warnings and what has happened since then? Undoubtedly many good things as David Lambert will show: the founding of the Civic Trust and the setting up of the Joint Committee of National Amenity Societies; English Heritage, Historic Scotland and Cadw: Welsh Historic Monuments; the Countryside Commission, the Nature Conservancy, the National Heritage Memorial Fund and the Heritage Lottery Fund; green belts, national parks, conservation areas, nature reserves, the

Victorian Society, SAVE, the Garden History Society, the urban parks programme, two and a half million members of the National Trust. But what of Clough Williams-Ellis's Beast? Is he now tamed? Is indignation a thing of the past? Is our heritage in safe hands? Far from it. Today's environment is still under threat with the increasing loss of buildings, landscapes, habitats, regional characteristics and tranquil areas.

This book is divided into three chapters. The first deals with the past, the early days of the amenity movement and the relevance of its Ruskinian origins. The second considers the situation today, and looks at what new approaches might be made to take the perception of heritage in the modern world out of its present backwater and into the political mainstream. The third sets out, with reference to two successful recent projects, how indignation can be channelled through community participation into a creative force for the future.

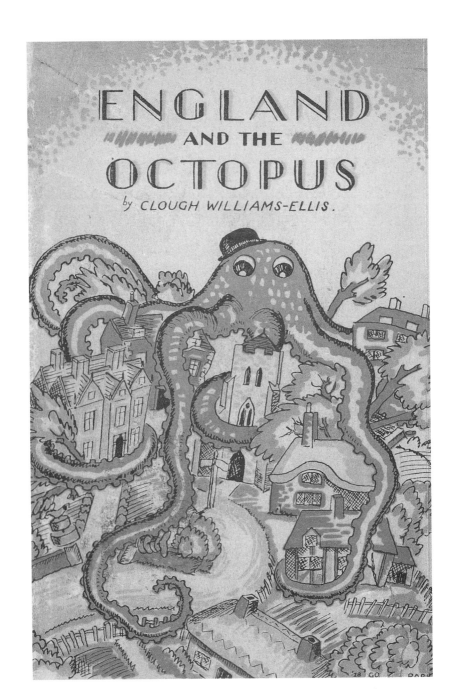

The jacket for Clough Williams-Ellis's *England and the Octopus* published in 1928

MAVIS BATEY

Ruskin, Morris and the early campaigns

JOHN RUSKIN (1819–1900) was the greatest moral authority and prophet of the nineteenth century, and his influence on education, politics, art and the environment is still significant in his centenary year. 'To see clearly', he said, 'is poetry, prophecy and religion – all in one'. His clarion calls, couched in powerfully compelling prose, were assiduously copied down in countless notebooks all over the world. In Tolstoy's words,

> Ruskin was one of the most remarkable men, not only in England and our time but of all countries and of all times. He was one of those rare men who think with their hearts and so he thought and said not only what he himself had seen and felt, but what everyone will think and say in the future.[1]

Heritage and tradition get in the way for most modern Utopians, but for Ruskin and his disciple William Morris the historic environment of monuments and landscape was a combination of art and living history essential for the quality of life. Both men were ahead of their time and in the progressive Victorian era saw themselves as guardians of change; they had an agenda for stewardship and sustainability which anticipated today's global concern for the environment. Ruskin provided the authority for protecting the environment, both manmade and natural, which inspired the amenity movement, as it would later become known, and gave it its strength. It was the enthusiasm and energies of his disciples which would set it going.

For Morris Ruskin was a prophet whose teaching was a new religion which he embraced whole-heartedly. When Morris was up at Oxford in the early 1850s he was still under the influence of the Oxford High Church Movement. He and Burne-Jones cast longing looks down the road at Newman's Littlemore oratory and in their holier moments planned to found their own monastery. 'This did not last long', Morris said, 'as it was corrected by the books of John Ruskin which were at the time a sort of revelation to me and seemed to point to a new road in which the world should travel'.[2] Ruskin had come to the rescue with vital new substitutes for Matthew Arnold's 'lost causes',[3] so leaving the missionary zeal of the Oxford Movement in place. Causes became crusades for William Morris and he lived up to his creed that 'every man who has a cause at heart must act as if it depended on him'.[4] Causes could be brought together to transform the 'art of living'. For Octavia Hill, also a fervent Ruskin disciple, 'causes are like stakes which are driven into a marsh and buried but carry the roadway'.[5]

The first Ruskinian cause was a holy war against the industrial age which had ushered in mass production, the degradation of the worker in the factory system and Mr Gradgrind with his market forces in Dickens's *Hard Times*. Ruskin, addressing a group of wealthy industrialists at Bradford remonstrated, 'But look strictly into the nature of the power of your Goddess of Getting on and you will find she is a Goddess – not of everybody's getting on – but of somebody's getting on'. His own philosophy engraved by his college on his memorial stone in Christ Church cathedral says it all: THERE IS NO WEALTH BUT LIFE.[6]

When Morris went up to Oxford *Modern Painters* and *The Seven Lamps of Architecture* had already been published, but it was *The Stones of Venice*, the second volume of which appeared in Morris's second year at Exeter College, that really brought Ruskin's ideas on art and society to his attention. In the chapter on 'The Nature of Gothic' Ruskin showed how the vitality and creative deeds of Venice were reflected in its decorative architecture, where the gothic craftsman had recorded every detail of life, with ingenuity and humour, in stark contrast to the stereotype designs by his classical counterpart. Ruskin had scaled its buildings recording every last detail of decoration and in his eloquent prose highlighted the human and cultural interest of architecture which had hitherto been seen as a coldly antiquarian study. For Ruskin art in its wider sense was an instrument for the welfare and happiness of mankind.

The idea of living history and the need to change society was a romantic revelation to Morris. In 1892 he would republish 'The Nature of Gothic' on his Kelmscott Press because, as he said, it was 'one of the very few necessary and inevitable utterances of the century'. These were the utterances on art and society with their moral and ethical substance which Morris and Burne-Jones had read over and over together as undergraduates; they permeated all Morris's lectures on the art of living and inspired his social concern for the welfare of the worker. 'You must either make a tool of the creature or a man of him'.[7] Ruskin's electrifying utterances continued to be a beacon of light for generations of students. Even in 1920 the young Kenneth Clark could write that it was no wonder that 'The Nature of Gothic' had had such a profound and immediate effect when even in his day, when the ideas it expressed were accepted, 'we cannot read it without a thrill, without a sudden resolution to reform the world'.[8]

Morris, in Ruskin's words, was not only a 'conceiver but a doer',[9] and it was Morris who, guided by Ruskin's 'lamps', would actively arouse public opinion to take up the cause of living in harmony with the past and protecting 'the sacred monuments of the nation's hope and growth'. For Morris, a poet at heart, romance was part of his being and he reminded members of the Society for the Protection of Ancient Buildings, which he formed in 1877 with Ruskin as a founder member, that 'what romance means is the capacity for a true conception of history for making the past part of the present'.[10] For Morris Pre-Raphaelite 'Truth to Nature' and its mood of spirituality was added to the exciting concept of living history. For Ruskin 'Truth to Nature' went deeper to include natural history, botany and geology.

When Ruskin was appointed Slade Professor of Art in 1869 he gave his popular lectures in the University Museum of Natural History which had been his brain-child. Art was of course wide-ranging for Ruskin, who maintained that the teaching of art was the teaching of all things and was dangerous unless grafted on to something deeper.[11] His audience knew that whatever the title of his lecture it would include art, architecture, geology, natural history, social justice, and his environmental concerns. His inaugural lecture called for the under-graduates to accept their social responsibilities. Thirteen years later, after Morris had been made an Honorary Fellow of Exeter College, he delivered a lecture on 'Art and Plutocracy' with Ruskin in the chair, at which he repeated the professor's teaching,

> I must ask you to extend the word Art beyond those matters which are consciously works of art... to extend it to the aspect of all the externals of our life – every one of the things that goes to make up the surroundings in which we live.[11]

Morris chose the fringe Cotswold village of Kelmscott as the 'earthly paradise' in which to pursue his Arts and Crafts ideology. Kelmscott was eulogised in his Utopian novel *News from Nowhere* where he tells us he immediately felt a sense of belonging to this old house by the Thames which had 'grown up out of the soil and the lives of the people who had lived in it'. Morris became a close friend of Edwin Austen Abbey, one of a team of illustrators sent over by *Harper's Monthly Magazine* to depict the English scene. This American colony of artists and writers had settled in Broadway and embarked on a sentimental discovery of their roots. Morris's Cotswolds satisfied their cravings for the English myth. Henry James, who met Morris, wrote of these passionate pilgrims in an article on 'Our Artists in Europe' for *Harper's Monthly Magazine*,

> Deep in their souls a natural affection answered to the England that the American imagination restricted to itself constructs from the poets, novelists and all the delightful testimony it inherits.[12]

Morris's second Ruskinian cause was that of preservation. As he was driving a party of friends to Broadway in 1876 the sight of Burford church being pulled down for 'restoration' infuriated him and he called for united action. The Society for the Protection of Ancient Buildings was founded the next year. He was fortunate in saving Inglesham church which bears a plaque to record that it had been 'restored' with the sensitive and loving treatment Morris had advocated. The SPAB had significant impact on the Kelmscott area, where Morris organised fund-raising appeals. He was instrumental in saving the Great Coxwell barn, which he said was the 'finest piece of architecture in England... as beautiful as a cathedral, yet with no ostentation of the builder's art'.[13] He protested to the Thames Conservancy about a proposal to rebuild a lock keeper's cottage near Kelmscott in red brick and Welsh slate instead of local materials.

When Ruskin settled into Brantwood on Lake Coniston in 1871, which was, like Morris's Kelmscott, his earthly paradise, he was equally appreciative of the vernacular architecture and the sense of place. He also found he could 'go to Nature in all singleness of heart' and develop his ideas on the interaction between man and nature. His woodland garden would show 'wild Nature tamed but not degraded under the hand of man'. He made plans for Guild of St George allotments and agricultural work to give 'knowledge of plants as you may best use in the country in which you live'; fuel should not be wasted on 'making plants blossom in winter' and he believed that 'without such unseasonable blossoms we would enjoy the Spring twice as much as now'.[14]

Both Ruskin and Morris saw that man was part of an ecosystem and appreciated the need for biodiversity and what is now called 'local distinctiveness'. They pleaded for native trees and not conifers to be planted, for native plants and nature reserves, the protection of birds and retention of hedgerows and verges; they condemned the artificiality of florists' flowers and the bigger the better flower show mentality, and thought that exotics, needing hot houses, should only be grown in botanic gardens. Morris remonstrated with the

Thames Conservancy for slashing the river banks and denuding them of water plants. Both Morris and Ruskin understood about water and air pollution and it seems that Ruskin had even foreseen the greenhouse effect; they stressed the need for sustainability with organic self-reliant communities using traditionally durable craft products.

Resuming his professorial duties in 1874 Ruskin organised his most famous environmental project. Believing that the energies of young undergraduates should be diverted from rowing to social schemes, he took out a gang in flannels with picks and barrows to make a new cart road at Ferry Hinksey, outside Oxford. The banks of the road were to be sown with wild flowers and the locals were to be persuaded to keep geese and donkeys on the green with small prizes offered for well-kept doorsteps and the cultivation of moss. The road was a disaster as the only good work was done by Ruskin's own gardener. The enterprise was, however, successful in generating Ruskin disciples at the Balliol breakfasts that followed.

Ruskin would later say,

> It is now the fashion to sneer at those Hinksey digging days but it will be found that many of the diggers who have helped in their time in social movements, in the improvement of dwellings of the poor in university setttlements in big towns and the like probably owe their interests in such matters to the spirit gleaned on our Hinksey dig.[15]

Arnold Toynbee was one such in the field of social and educational improvements, but another disciple, Hardwicke Rawnsley was motivated in a different way and maintained close links with his master in the Lake District when he became vicar of Crosthwaite, near Keswick, and a leading light of the Wordsworth Society. Appropriately it was Wordsworth's influence which cemented their relationship when the new cause of landscape preservation was fostered.

Ruskin greatly admired Wordsworth, whom he said he 'used as a daily text book from youth to age and have lived moreover in all essential facts according to the tenor of his teaching'.[16] There was an 'exquisite rightness' in Wordsworth's poetry of nature, but Ruskin's thoughts for preserving the landscape that he extolled derived from the poet's *Guide to the Lakes*. Published in 1810, it was a far cry from the previous picturesque tours and urged that those who lived in the Lakes had a duty to see that their houses belonged to the landscape in harmony with nature. Ruskin achieved this goal when he retired to Brantwood in the 1870s.

It was at an early meeting of the Wordsworth Society, with Ruskin and Rawnsley present and Matthew Arnold in the chair, that the Lake District Defence Society was formed to resist development in Wordsworth's beloved landscape in the 1880s. Wordsworth had given both Ruskin and Morris a new perception of collective landscape and a sense of public involvement without ownership when he described in his *Guide to the Lakes* 'a sort of national property in which every man has a right and interest, who has an eye to perceive and a heart to enjoy'. This sense of poetic appropriation without ownership was taken to America by Ralph Waldo Emerson, who met Wordsworth in 1832, and later heard Ruskin lecture. In 'Nature' he wrote,

> The charming landscape which I saw this morning is made up of some twenty or thirty farms. Miller owns this field, Locke that, and Manning the woodland beyond... but none of them owns the landscape... There is a property on the far horizon, which no man has but he whose eye can integrate all the parts, that is the poet.[17]

At the time that Morris was discovering the Cotswolds with a true sense of place and of belonging, a local guide echoed Emerson's sentiments: 'It matters not who owns this house or that field, the landscape is ours, it is free to all who care to linger and look at its beauty'. Morris, who had already seen the necessity for a cause for campaigning for ancient buildings, took Wordsworth's perception of public landscape to the inevitable further stage of preservation: 'When you have accepted the maxim that the external aspect of the country belongs to the whole public and that whatever wilfully injures that property is a public enemy the cause will be on its way'.[18]

Rawnsley took the cause of preservation even further and was instrumental in promoting the idea of acquiring and holding land in trust for the public. The battles of the 1870s to preserve Open Spaces, such as Epping Forest and Hampstead Heath, had highlighted the need for a body to hold open spaces in perpetuity with legislative powers. Sir Robert Hunter, the hero of the Open Spaces movement, was the co-founder of the National Trust with Rawnsley and Octavia Hill. Truly in keeping with Ruskin's 'lamps' of beauty and memory the National Trust was founded in 1895 for 'places of natural beauty and historic interest'. Rawnsley wished to put it on record that 'it was Ruskin's teaching which was the fountain head of the teaching which set forward the National

Trust'. The first major Lake District acquisition was Brandelhow Park on Lake Derwentwater opposite the memorial Rawnsley had erected at Friars Crag to his master. The appeal leaflet for Brandelhow Park was headed to 'all lovers of Ruskin' and at the opening in 1902 Octavia Hill rejoiced that 'it will be preserved in its present loveliness and it belongs to you all and to every landless man, woman and child in England'

The twentieth century would need more than Ruskin's moral authority and 'lamp of beauty' to guide it. Ruskin disliked committees, legal practicalities and lobbying – a shortcoming which Octavia Hill was rash enough to point out to him. She was convinced, however, he would remain inspirational but would not be able to give practical leads to the new century which he only lived a fortnight to see. 'They were brilliant lamps enough', as Clough Williams-Ellis observed, 'but as practical guiding lights they were too dazzling… and not showing the plain man the path he was to tread'.[19] In the 1890s it was becoming increasingly apparent that *laissez-faire* development could not go unchecked and that professional institutions and legislation would have to promote town and country planning. The problem was most acute in London where development was extending at an alarming rate down the rural Thames.

Once travel became easy it was not long before people were inspired to build houses to take advantage of Wordsworth's Lakes, Matthew Arnold's 'Scholar Gypsy' view of Oxford and Turner and Thomson's Arcadian image of the 'matchless vale of Thames'.[20] Saving the view from Richmond Hill, made famous by Turner, became a *cause célèbre* at the end of the century. The first intimation of the iniquity of *laissez-faire* came in 1898 when the *Thames Valley Times* reported that Mr Glover, the boatman who owned the small island in the foreground of the view, had threatened to sell it as a site for advertising hoardings. There was much local 'indignation' and the national organisation SCAPA, formed in 1893 as the Society for Checking the Abuses of Public Advertising, rallied in support. It called on the nation to respond to the local appeal to buy Glover's Island to which 'Professor Ruskin' had donated a guinea.

The view was to be threatened with even greater development in 1901 and legislation would be needed to prevent it. A housing estate was proposed in the grounds of the famous riverside villa of Marble Hill. In 1901 there was no legislation to protect Marble Hill as an historic building and far less to place restrictions on developing its 66 acre landscape. Epping Forest and Hampstead Heath had both been saved from development in the 1870s by Acts of Parliament but these were open spaces issues; saving a view in perpetuity was rather different.

But a new feeling of national heritage was abroad in 1901 largely thanks to the National Trust and the preservation societies. The London papers took up Richmond's cause as an instance of national heritage and lamented that its fate was in the hands of speculative builders and unenlightened local councils too often on their side.

Following grassroots pressure from the Commons and Footpaths Preservation Society, the Kyrle Society, the Thames Preservation League, the Metropolitan Public Gardens Association and the National Trust, the London County Council agreed that every effort should be made to save the world famous view and called a meeting at County Hall. The first step was to acquire the Marble Hill estate through their General Powers Act of 1898 which had enabled the London County Council to acquire property. A bill, for which there was no legal precedent, would have to follow to safeguard the rest of the riverside land, on both sides of the river, from development in the future. Fortunately Sir Robert Hunter, the honorary solicitor of the Commons and Footpaths Preservation Society, who had been knighted in 1894 for his services to the open spaces movement, was on hand to guide.

The CFPS had been formed in 1865 to resist illegal encroachment of common land, and was the inspiration for effective and principled campaigning. Its founder and chairman, the MP George Shaw-Lefevre, also agreed to serve on the Richmond Hill view executive committee. Robert Hunter was officially solicitor for the Post Office, for whom he drafted over fifty successful bills, but at home in Haslemere he worked tirelessly with the paperwork for good environmental causes. Henry Fawcett, the Post Master General, commented that he had never known a professional man who had done so much professional work for nothing. As a founder of the National Trust with Rawnsley and Octavia Hill, and its chairman until his death in 1912, he steered the constitution through the legal procedures and was responsible for the invaluable concept of 'inalienable land' in the 1907 Act; as honorary solicitor to the Kyrle Society, which was also represented on the Richmond committee, he assisted Octavia Hill in many of her social welfare schemes. He was also a keen supporter of public parks and the Metropolitan Public Gardens Association, formed in 1882, which was also represented on the Richmond committee.

Nature conservation called for a different form of indignation as it was largely the naturalists themselves who had to be converted – from guns to binoculars. Collecting and classifying was the discipline they followed and a bird was only identified by being shot. The 1860s' women's fashion for feathers also spurred the Revd F.O.Morris, a correspondent of Ruskin's, to write indignation letters to *The Times*, but it was not until 1880 that the Wild Birds Protection Act was passed.[21] Nature conservation appealed to those nurtured on Wordsworth and the romantic poets and when the Selborne Society was founded in 1886 for the 'Preservation of Birds, Plants and Pleasant Places' it invited Tennyson to become its president. The founding of the Royal Society for the Protection of Birds took place three years later.

SCAPA, already mentioned in connection with its opposition to hoardings on the Thames, as all the other nineteenth-century 'causes', saw its remit as wider than that implied in its title. Disfigurement of surroundings was always a primary concern. 'We want to make the daily journey from home to office or workshop, which forms a large part of the outdoor life of many of our people, as refreshing and as little irksome as the necessary conditions of modern society permit'.[22] Checking abuses in public advertising was all part of the wider issue of 'the protection of the amenities of aspect in our country' which they saw as 'a public interest in the same sense as the defence of our shores'. When SCAPA was absorbed into the CPRE in 1926 that organisation gratefully acknowledged its debt to the society which had 'first begun to look after the country generally'.[23] SCAPA's first president, the architect Alfred Waterhouse, and his wife were devotees of Ruskin's 'lamp of beauty' and Mrs Waterhouse proposed that their new cause should be called 'The Beautiful World Society'; this was rejected in favour of SCAPA but their magazine would be called *The Beautiful World*.

The secretary of SCAPA, Richardson Evans, like Robert Hunter a gentle but persuasive eco-warrior, set up the first local amenity society as such, in 1903, at Wimbledon, where he lived. Admittedly the Sid Vale Association began as early as 1846 but this at the time was specifically for the enhancement of the promenades and footpaths of the seaside resort of Sidmouth for the benefit of citizens and visitors; it later became a civic amenity society and still flourishes today. The Cockburn Association was also founded as a popular organisation as early as 1875 to preserve and increase the attractions of Edinburgh. From small beginnings it developed later into the Edinburgh Civic Trust, the premier local conservation body in Scotland. Evans called his Wimbledon society after the early environmentalist John Evelyn, just as Octavia Hill had named her Kyrle Society after Pope's civically-minded John Kyrle, the Man of Ross, and the Selborne Society had been named in honour of the famous nineteenth-century naturalist Gilbert White who lived there. Evelyn seems to have been the first person to associate the word amenity with landscape.

Richardson Evans wanted the John Evelyn Club of Wimbledon to combine its social village club function with concern for the local amenities and to be the 'guardian genius' of the area. Following Ruskin's quasi-religious example at Sheffield he also saw the need to include a museum to encourage interest in nature, a library of local books and a collection of old engravings to encourage local identity. He wanted this to be an example of how a local society could 'cover the whole field of the finer amenities' and maintained that 'our movement is essentially religious. By religion, I mean that sense of reverence for man and nature and that feeling of obligation to strive for the well-being of others'. He saw this Ruskinian aim as 'an organic whole' with SCAPA and urged that a network of amenity associations could 'form a non-party political force that will be more than a match for the Philistines'.[24]

Another strong force to combat the philistines was the university extension movement. Mechanics Institutes had been set up in the first half of the century to teach skills to artisans in the new industrial age. The courses provided by university extension teaching were non-vocational and offered wide-ranging liberal and social studies to all. When Prince Leopold, a pupil of Ruskin's, gave a speech in support of the London Society for the Extension of University Teaching in 1879 he welcomed it as an encouragement to the understanding and appreciation of the environment,

> Of such aims we in Oxford have had a great and inspiring example... the power of drawing the full measure of instruction and happiness from the wonderful world on which rich and poor can gaze alike.

In 1898 all the societies concerned with the environment held a conference and called on the House of Commons to set up an 'Amenities Committee' which would work out a strategy for local government; with their dedicated grass-roots campaigning for open spaces, public parks, ancient buildings, better housing and land in trust, the CFPS, the Kyrle Society, the SPAB, SCAPA, the Metropolitan Public Gardens Association and the National Trust had been the bedrock of the amenity movement. Sir Robert Hunter with his unrivalled conservation lobbying and legal expertise had been a tower of strength; assembling his papers, now in the Surrey History Centre at Woking, must have been a trial, although a labour of love, for his family.[25]

Octavia Hill's Kyrle Society still had the truly Ruskinian stated desire 'to bring the refining and cheerful influences of natural and artistic beauty home to the people'; however, the more practical planning words 'amenity' and 'national heritage' would soon replace Ruskin's visionary lamps of beauty and of memory. The first time the word 'amenity' as a legal concept appeared was in the Housing and Town Planning Act of 1909. Promoted with the genuine intention of providing better housing and slum clearance, the bill proposed to give local authorities powers of compulsory purchase of land for the purpose. Admirable as this might sound to Octavia Hill, who cared so deeply about social housing issues, she and Sir Robert Hunter saw the need to control comprehensive housing development and with the other preservation societies argued that 'open spaces in both Urban and Rural districts are fully as important to the working classes and other inhabitants as any other provision for their welfare'.[26]

When the bill was enacted in 1909 provisions were therefore made in town planning for public 'amenity'. Full advantage would be taken of Section 24 which stated that 'foremost amongst the matters which should be regarded as coming under the general heading of amenity is the preservation of places of natural beauty… and historical interest'. Writing for the newly formed National Housing and Town Planning Council, Fred Pearce, the Twickenham borough surveyor who had been involved in the battle to save Marble Hill, urged that now so much responsibility was placed on the local authority for the 'amenity of the area' it was the duty of the citizens to become vigilant and remind local authorities of their powers and opportunities. Ruskin had called for a national network of 'observers' to give an early warning of historic buildings at risk some fifty years before and Morris had set up a few local SPAB 'watching' committees, but it was now imperative that all the citizens should be aware of their responsibilities for conservation.

With this in mind amenity societies began to be set up all over the country. These did not, after all, follow the example of Richardson Evans's Wimbledon Society, which required an establishment; the early amenity societies often conducted their business in private homes. The Bath Preservation Society was one of the first to be set up in 1910 following an indignation meeting held in the Assembly Rooms to protest against a clear case of municipal vandalism. The Bristol Civic Society was not founded until 1946 but had evolved from the Bristol Kyrle Society, set up in 1905 with Octavia Hill's ideas of influencing 'what is most beautiful in nature and art', but now seen as inadequate for a pressure group. The Oxford Preservation Society was formed in the 1920s by Michael Sadler for the 'preservation of the amenities of the city of Oxford and its surroundings'. Sadler was a Ruskin disciple and prime mover of Oxford University extension courses. One of his first tasks was to preserve Matthew Arnold's 'Scholar Gypsy' view from Cumnor Hill, then threatened by development.[27]

Patrick Abercrombie, the pioneer town planner, who more than anyone else was responsible for bringing the concept of 'amenity' into general use, was the inspiration of the Council for the Preservation of Rural England in 1926. He had pointed out that local authorities had failed to realise that their powers concerning 'amenity' in the town planning section of the 1909 Act could also apply to rural preservation. The CPRE's remit was for the preservation of the amenity of the whole countryside. As its first secretary Abercrombie said,

> We speak eloquently of the obligation that is on us to preserve and save from destruction the ancient monuments of this land, visible signs of our history, but we are apt to forget that the greatest historical monument we possess, the most essential thing which is England, is the Countryside, the Market Town, the Village, the Hedgerow trees, the lanes, the copses, the streams and farmstead.[28]

Similar organisations were set up in Wales and Scotland.

We have today lost touch with those clear clarion calls for a holistic approach to the care of the environment and for our responsibilities as custodians and trustees of the national heritage.[29] The millennium slogan has been 'forward-looking Britain', but there is an urgent need for the national amenity societies to speak again with one voice to demonstrate in clear Ruskinian terms 'how everything blends together' in Morris's concern for 'every one of the things that goes to make up the surroundings in which we live'.

The national conservation societies play a vital role in lobbying government and providing umbrellas for their various causes; the Civic Trust for affiliated civic societies; the national association for the county naturalist trusts and the CPRE for co-ordinating the work of their regional branches. Valuable as they are, it is the local amenity societies which Richardson Evans saw as the guardians of the genius of the place, who can best advance the 'causes' of environmental conservation and regeneration at grassroots level. When the Minister of Culture, Media and Sport, Chris Smith, launched the new Local Heritage Initiative, backed by lottery funding, in February 2000, he recognised that 'the long term future of our local heritage lies in the hands of those who value it at local level'. As well as the local authorities concerned, and particularly the schools, it is the local amenity societies and interest groups who have such a vital role to play today in cherishing and enhancing their surroundings.

There is still much need for 'indignation' meetings, but in Evans's words to his first amenity society at Wimbledon, 'If the Local Associations are to be a pioneer for good they must try to cover the whole field of the finer amenities, to devote themselves to constructive work as well as preventive and cultivate the municipal spirit'.[30] It is the fostering of this sense of place and community whereby we can see ourselves fitting into the world that is so essential to the quality of life that Ruskin, Morris, Octavia Hill, Robert Hunter, Richardson Evans, Patrick Abercrombie and the other pioneers of the amenity movement were striving for.

English Heritage's Historic Environment Review, commissioned by the Department of Culture, Media and Sport, should bring all the current ideas into focus. In the welcome invitation for national amenity societies to participate in the review comes the statement, 'Horizons have broadened, as have aspirations for the heritage and the role it plays in modern life'. All the organisations will be studying the findings with interest to see how they can best be guardians of change. As pressure groups have proliferated in the last decades of the century there has been a tendency for each to fight its own patch, whereas the strength of the early amenity movement was the power in combination exerted by separate motivations or 'causes'. It is interesting to recall, however, that all the new concepts of sustainability, local distinctiveness, social inclusion and the quality of life to be debated in the review were implicit in the Ruskinian origins of the amenity movement.

1   For Tolstoy and Ruskin see Derrick Leon, *Tolstoy: His Life and Work* (1949), p.303. Quotation given in Brantwood guide.

2   *Letters*, ed. P.Henderson (1950), pp.184–86. See also Morris's Preface to *The Nature of Gothic* (1892).

3   Matthew Arnold, *Essays in Criticism* (1865).

4   'The Art and Beauty of the Earth', *Collected Works* (24 Vols, 1910–15), ed. May Morris, Vol. 22, p.174.

5   Gillian Darley, *Octavia Hill* (1990), p.212.

6   E.T.Cook and Alexander Wedderburn, *The Library Edition of the Works of John Ruskin* (1903–12), Vol.18, p.452 and Vol.17, p.105.

7   John Ruskin, *The Stones of Venice*, 'The Nature of Gothic', Vol.II, xii.

8   Kenneth Clark, *The Gothic Revival* (1962), p.186.

9   John Ruskin, *Works*, Vol.33, p.390.

10 SPAB Annual General Meeting, 3 July 1889.

11 William Morris, *Works*, Vol.23, p.164.

12 Henry James, 'Our Artists in Europe', *Harper's Monthly Magazine* (1889), p.58.

13 P.Henderson, William Morris, his Life, Work and Friends (1967), p.225.

14 John Ruskin, *Works*, Vol.28, p.182.

15 Darley, op.cit. p.36; note 36. See also *Atlantic Monthly*, Vol.85, pp.572–76.

16 John Ruskin, *Works*, Vol.34, p.349.

17 R.W.Emerson, *Essays* (1844), Chapter 1, 'Nature'.

18 William Morris, *Collected Works*, 'The Art and Beauty of the Earth', Vol.22, p.173.

19 Clough Williams-Ellis, *England and the Octopus* (1928), p.183.

20 See Batey, Buttery, Lambert and Wilkie, *Arcadian Thames* (1997).

21 See D.Elliston Allen, *The Naturalist in Britain* (1976), p.198.

22 From 'SCAPA: Why it exists. What it may hope to do' (1896), paper by Richardson Evans.

23 Clough Williams-Ellis, op. cit., p.186.

24 R.Evans and C.Arnold, 'The John Evelyn Idea', *Wimbledon and Merton Annual* (1903), p.140.

25 Papers of Sir Robert Hunter, 1621/– , Surrey History Centre, Woking.

26 Hunter papers, 1621 Box 12/5. A submission from the CFPS, MPGA, Kyrle Society and the National Trust during the passage of the 1909 Housing and Town Planning Bill.

27 Matthew Arnold revived Glanvill's story of *The Scholar Gypsy* and its memories in *Thyrsis*. When *Rambles with Matthew Arnold* appeared in 1908 many literary pilgrims sought out the sites up Boars Hill and when the land came up for sale in the 1920s speculative builders lost no time in catering for the pilgrims who wanted to live on 'the beloved hillside'.

28 See Patrick Abercrombie, *The Preservation of Rural England* (1926).

29 See Ruskin's creed on custodianship quoted in the Introduction, p.7, as set out in 'The Lamp of Memory' (1849), *Works*, Vol.8, p.233. Also Morris to the SPAB General meeting, 1879, 'We are only custodians and trustees... our bounden duty is to hand on unimpaired to posterity the priceless heritage as we have received it'.

30 Letter from Richardson Evans, November 1921, EPH 1 333. The SCAPA papers are deposited at the Wimbledon Society Museum, formerly the John Evelyn Club of Wimbledon.

THE PRESERVED AMENITY

Thomas Derrick's cartoon for *Punch* 1937.
Conservation has been easy to mock for most of the twentieth century.

DAVID LAMBERT

Indignation today

The cause of conservation is today at a turning point. It has travelled from honourable origins in the socially aware campaigning of William Morris, John Ruskin and the founders of the National Trust, the CPRE and the Ramblers' Association, through a variety of more elitist phases, into fairly widespread discredit. There are, however, now great opportunities to redeem its name and to chart an honourable course into the future. A guide to that course, to understanding the meaning of 'heritage' and to furthering the relationship between conservation and development, can be found in the experience of the early days of the amenity movement.

As described in the previous chapter, a sense of legitimate public interest in privately owned property is at the root of Britain's unique heritage of amenity societies and other voluntary pressure groups. Although local amenity societies were being formed from the earliest days of the twentieth century, the formation of the Civic Trust in 1957 formally signalled their arrival, and spurred on their growth. From 200 in that year their numbers rose to 600 by 1967; over 300,000 people now belong to their local civic society. The Architectural Heritage Fund's founding in 1975 had the same effect on building preservation trusts, whose numbers rose from 15 in that year to 148 today. There is an amenity society for every type of building, from fountains to cinemas, and for countless towns and neighbourhoods. There are global organisations such as Friends of the Earth and Greenpeace which are also active at a local level. And of course the greatest phenomenon in environmentalism in the past twenty years has been the rise of the *ad hoc*, single-issue, direct action groupings, which thrived on the sense of disenfranchisement among the young and their passionate determination to fight the establishment; a sense of being outsiders which is a key to all the above pressure groups but which manifested itself in for example the Newbury bypass protest in a dramatic form.

This public interest in private property, and the formation of such groups, seems to be unique to Britain – a place which ironically has resisted all assaults on private property. But this is a small island in which we are crowded together: what one individual does affects others –whether it be closing moors in order to shoot grouse or putting in uPVC windows.

This public interest is described in the latest, the only, Government guidance on the historic environment, *Planning Policy Guidance* note 15 (1994). It opens by giving reasons for the preservation of the physical remnants of the past: it cites their contribution to 'our cultural heritage and our sense of national identity' (two highly charged and ambiguous concepts); it cites their being an 'irreplaceable educational record', their immense contribution to 'leisure and recreation', and – it comes second –

> Their presence adds to the quality of our lives, by enhancing the familiar and cherished local scene and sustaining the sense of local distinctiveness which is so important an aspect of the character and appearance of our towns, villages and countryside.[1]

It is a fascinating statement, and my fascination focuses on the use of the word 'cherished'. The more one considers it, the more anomalous it seems, for it shortcircuits all notions of supposedly objective assessment, judicious centralised analysis, grading and quantification, and introduces the powerful, irrational element of emotion (rather than judgement), in those who see a place so often that it is familiar and well-loved.

Heritage, if it is 'ours', cannot be determined from a single, central, bird's-eye perspective. It is multi-faceted, resistant to ordering, possessed of its own 'dimension and density',[2] and the inevitable attempt to order it leaves out myriad things and places which people value. And that is where the amenity society, the outsider, opposing the establishment and vested interest, comes in. Anyone who has been involved in campaigning knows that it is the personal sense of *indignation* at a threat to what is *cherished* which is the fuel that burns within all resistance to what is perceived as harmful change. The older elements in a place are generally the focus of what we cherish: continuity with the past is the source of the kind of emotional and psychic stability to which all humans respond. Conservation is thus often far from a minority, academic interest in preserving data about the past, but is on the contrary a deep-rooted, inherently radical, instinct with a strong populist strain. If it is to tap that strain, then the heritage establishment needs to recognise the enormous range of things and places people value.

If we acknowledge that a shack can be *valued* as highly as a mediaeval bridge, we do not open the proverbial and dreaded floodgates, we get – like bankrupt aristocrats marrying into American heiresses in the twenties – an injection of new blood and energy. The preservationist urge is widespread, deep-rooted, powerful: to alienate train-spotters, Broads-Cruiser devotees, allotment enthusiasts, and bungalow fanatics, is – philosophically – to deny the richness of that urge and – opportunistically – to miss out on tapping a hugely populist and politically powerful strain in British culture.

'Heritage is dead', was the conclusion of an article in the *Sunday Telegraph* in 1998, and the article described the general sense that the big battles for what the public and heritage consensus agrees are historic buildings are over: legislation does now protect everything worth protecting. The article was written by Ken Powell, director of the Twentieth Century Society, and his argument was that there are still battles to be fought, but as always on the margins, the territory's borders, its frontline, in this case, post-war buildings.[3]

The same applies to historic gardens. The first edition of the *Register of Historic Parks and Gardens in England* was completed in 1988, with a heavy emphasis on eighteenth-century rural landscape parks. Except for a handful, such as People's Park in Halifax, nineteenth-century urban parks were viewed as an interesting phenomenon but not worth registering – the Scottish *Inventory* left them out altogether. Since then, with the publication of Hazel Conway's *People's Parks* in 1990, their importance has begun to be recognised and about 120 have now been registered. At ten per cent of the total this is still too few properly to reflect their importance, and registering is still hamstrung by the vexed question of condition – Philips and Queens Parks in Manchester, for example, surely merit registering, despite their run-down appearance, for their historic importance, as the first laid out by public subscription to designs by Joshua Major in 1846.

Many of the arguments about conservation today are familiar echoes from the debates a hundred years ago. The early days of the CPRE especially seem to be full of relevance today. First, it was seen as retrograde and was defended from the charge vigorously: Anthony Bertram in his 1938 Penguin Special on *Design* wrote,

> There is a grossly unfair tendency to mix up the CPRE with the sort of arid conservatism which tries to mummify the countryside, which automatically opposes all innovations, all new design, all demolition and reconstruction. If any such people hide under the cloak of the CPRE, they have certainly no right to be there.[4]

Preservation in the twenties and thirties aligned itself with modernisation, an alignment which also existed in the forties, when listing, for example, was set up to guide reconstruction rather than to resist it.[5]

Second, the CPRE was open to the charge of being autocratic. Patrick Abercrombie, the pioneering town planner, was the leading light of the CPRE at its founding, and vigorous planning was at its heart. While it stopped short of advocating the nationalisation of the land, it proposed not only National Parks, but a central Board of Planning and a Government Board of Scenery. The great enemy, as anyone who reads Clough Williams-Ellis's *England and the Octopus* (1928) will see, was the *laissez-faire* government, at local and national levels, that had allowed creeping suburbanisation, desecration of villages and road-sides and the sprawl of *ad hoc* development. The campaign for conservation was a highly autocratic movement, engineered by a handful of articulate individuals demanding control and restrictive government and impatient of other points of view.

Both these facts about the early days of the CPRE seem relevant today when faced with the caricature of planning, conservation, and amenity movements as, respectively, men in grey shoes with clip boards, fogies of all ages, and Nimbies. The difference is that in those early days preservation envisaged itself hand in hand with development to create a modern environment and society.

That very strong recognition by Williams-Ellis and others, that conservation meant Government action – or as it would be termed today, interference – is particularly telling. Since Mrs Thatcher's heady days of development corporations and infamously of 'lifting the burden' (i.e. of planning on developers), to the current Government's programme of 'modernising' planning, the drive to whittle away at planning has continued unabated.

We face a free-market free-for-all, in which embattled planners and conservationists face dog-fights against financially better-equipped opposition. Government professes itself helpless to resist the economic imperatives of global or continental market forces or trading agreements. But 4.4 million new homes are demanded – not needed – by 2016, while motorway use doubled in the nineteen-eighties and road traffic generally is predicted to grow between 35 and 70 per cent by 2020. Government action is needed now even more than in the thirties; setting down limits and constraints, imposing burdens, resisting mere free-market *demand* in favour of strong planning based on assessment of capacity and *need*.

The strength and danger inherent in all conservation is value judgement. Strength because it taps the deepest feelings in its promoters, of all sorts; there were passionate value judgements behind the preservation of the country house, as there are behind the road-protests of the mid-1990s or the preservation of a non-'important' park such as Cripplegate Park in Worcester, infamously dismissed by the leader of the city council as being of no importance because 'people just walk through it'. Danger, because of the inherent problems of such judgements being rooted in a specific temporal cultural context. For example, in the 1930s the pylons of the new National Grid were welcomed as of 'real beauty'.[6] Williams-Ellis lays into bandstands, tram-shelters, park gates, pavilions and public lavatories 'with their exuberant cast-iron arabesques and crestings and general dolled-up absurdity' and into park railings as 'disfiguring barriers' which we should uproot, unless, he asks with what is now an unintentional double irony, 'we in truth love them for their own sake and for all that they stand for and symbolise', to which of course now the answer generally is, yes: the Lottery is putting millions into replacing them to great public acclaim.[7] Similarly, it now seems pitiful that Williams-Ellis could write, 'There is surely something rather noble about the broad white concrete ribbons laid in sweeping curves and easy gradients across the country – something satisfying in their clean-planed cuttings and embankments'.[8] The autobahns of Germany were widely and passionately admired by preservationists and modernists alike.

Petrol stations in particular were anathema to preservationists. Harry Peach and Noel Carrington in *The Face of the Land* (1930) mocked the – as we now see it – wonderful half-timbered, pagoda-roofed petrol station in Beckenham, because of its lack of 'fitness for purpose'.[9] The building is now listed and described approvingly in the latest Pevsner as being in 'a rampant Road to Mandalay style'.[10] While we can all see the fatal flaw in a formula like 'fitness for purpose', the basis for our current appreciation of the building was simply unimaginable seventy years ago, and impossible to predict. It is not that our taste is corrupt or decadent, but the simple fact that value, as Hume and others told the eighteenth-century about beauty, derives not just from objects themselves but from its cultural context. Three contentions can be made in the light of this story.

First, the authoritarian, *faux*-objective nature of conservation remains its Achilles' heel. It is one of the chief reasons for its current marginalisation, equally distasteful to new Labour as it was to Mrs Thatcher's new Conservative. It is that which grates most on this reader in going over thirties texts with their notions of 'right leisure using', or of 'Cockney' visitors' 'flagrant breach of national good form'.[11] Williams-Ellis berated 'the intrusive impertinence of bungalows' although 'Cottabunga', the example illustrated in *England and the Octopus*, is probably rather appealing to modern eyes.[12] It is no wonder then that as he complained in *England and the Octopus*, 'As yet there is no general public opinion in favour of conservation, and that's the frightful and hamstringing truth'.[13]

Second, – going back to Hume – cultural context is largely but not entirely social, it is also unique and personal. The environmentalist Chris Baines traces his campaign for urban wilderness back to 'an early childhood played out on the bomb sites and abandoned allotments of post-war Sheffield... and... the weedy canals, recolonised clay pits and waste tips of the Black Country'.[14] Conservation is thus only progressive where the unique obsessions of its protagonists overlap with concerns shared more widely by others.

Third, conservation is not 'on behalf of' future generations. How can we know what those unborn individuals and structures will want to have preserved for them? The imagined prospect of children or children's children, unborn generations, enjoying everything we preserve and approving of everything we allow to be demolished, is commonly cited as justifying conservation. But how do we know that in the future the loss of inner-city allotments or unlisted thirties shacks will not be mourned and the preservation of eighteenth-century terrace facades scorned? The point is, we preserve first for ourselves, for the quality of our own life and environment, and for our own peace of mind: posterity is a false and unnecessary alibi.

The twentieth century has seen a constant jostling between what we might call elitist heritage, principally the country house preservation movement, and the common heritage. It becomes clear that the ascendancy of the former may actually prove to be a fairly brief phase. Even in 1954, in the middle of the decade which saw the peak of country-house demolition, John Harvey's call for 'a national sense of indigation' at 'the squandering of the country's patrimony now in progress', was about the loss of mediaeval and vernacular buildings rather than country houses.[15]

In 1927 the head of the Office of Works, Sir Lionel Earle, remarked that Britain had 'fewer provisions to preserve historic buildings than any other country in Europe, with the exception of Turkey and the Balkan states'.[16] But, pre-Second World War, there was little consensus on any form of preservation. In 1937 for example, the government rebuked countryside campaigners thus,

It is necessary to remember that the countryside is not the preserve of the wealthy and leisured classes. The country rightly prides itself on the fact that since the War there has been an unparalleled building development, a development which every Government has done its utmost to stimulate, and whose effect has been to create new and better social conditions for a very large number of persons.[17]

When listing was debated in the House of Commons in 1937, there was a call for it to include much more than just historic buildings. The architect MP Sir Alfred Bossom urged the Government to look at 'the destruction of beauty in town and country and the danger to houses of architectural or historic interest'; he urged the Government to begin a survey which would,

> reveal the monuments that could or should be saved; the villages, houses, cottages, churches, bridges, the hilltops, rivers, banks and woods, where roads should go and should not go, and where they should by-pass. In fact it could reveal the whole story of what we possess.[18]

It was in the same spirit that Chancellor Hugh Dalton set up the Land Fund after the war. Dalton, known as the Red Rambler of the Pennines, was president of the Ramblers' Association and a socialist, more at home in a Pennine pub than a stately home, and he had sought to establish a fund, using war surplus money, for the purchase of open land for public access. Dalton's Budget speech in the House of Commons, 9 April 1946, announcing the fund, called it a,

> thank-offering for victory, and a war memorial which, in the judgement of many, is better than any work of art in stone or bronze. I should like to think that through this Fund we shall dedicate some of the loveliest parts of this land to the memory of those who died in order that we might live in freedom... let this land of ours be dedicated to the memory of our dead, and to the use and enjoyment of the living for ever.

At this stage, there was little support for country-house preservation. James Lees-Milne, fighting an often despairing battle to acquire country houses for the National Trust epitomises the elitism which was so out of tune with the period, writing in 1946 of a house called Brockhampton,

> This evening the whole tragedy of England impressed itself upon me. This small, not very important seat in the heart of our secluded country, is now deprived of its last squire. A whole social system has broken down. What will replace it beyond government by the masses, uncultivated, rancourous, savage, philistine, the enemies of all things beautiful? How I detest democracy.[19]

However, in 1950, Sir Ernest Gowers published his report on the committee of inquiry into the question of country house preservation. This had been commissioned in the wake of Dalton's forced resignation and replacement with Sir Stafford Cripps, who was much less inclined towards the wider rural amenities which Dalton had in mind in setting up the Land Fund. The report took the traditional, *Country-Life*, line on the importance of country houses, and called for tax exemption for owners and grants from a new Historic Buildings Council.

But just as the pendulum may have been swinging towards country houses, the election was lost in 1951. The new Conservative government resented Gowers's proposals as more Labour-inspired state-planning, with the National Trust appearing as a kind of semi-nationalisation. Macmillan, the new planning minister, said, 'the fact must be faced that the mode of life for which these notable houses stood was doomed'.[20] Finally in 1953, resisted by the Conservative minister of works who was against 'turning ourselves into a nation of subsidised museum keepers', the Government announced a scaled-down version of the Labour proposals based on Gowers, and Parliament passed the Historic Buildings and Ancient Monuments Act.[21]

So when does elitist heritage come to the fore? Arguably, only as late as the seventies. In 1960 the National Trust had 100,000 members, in 1970 200,000 and then it takes off: over a million by 1980 and over two million in 1990. In 1993 over a third of the population visited a stately home.

The notion that the heritage of the social elite is a matter of concern for all is arguably a very recent phenomenon. As late as 1974 the Garden History Society eschewed aligning itself in its representations on the proposed Wealth Tax with the perceived vested interests of the Country Landowners' Association and Historic Houses Associaton, preferring instead to go in with the CPRE and the Footpaths Society, to show how much the character of the English countryside was endebted to the country house landscape. So how did this late rise of the country house above the environment as a whole come about?

Dismay about the dereliction of country houses came into sharp focus in the Victoria and Albert Museum exhibition *The Destruction of the Country House* in 1974. This was complemented by the Cornforth report for the British Tourist Authority, *Country Houses in Britain: can they survive?*, in the same year, and fortuitously perhaps by the new Labour government's alarming proposals for Capital Transfer Tax and a wealth tax. Public concern was galvanised by journalists and campaigners such as Marcus Binney, who was architectural correspondent for *Country Life* at the time and founded SAVE Britain's Heritage in 1975. SAVE's arguments were pitched in terms that anticipate sustainability by twenty years, arguing that re-use of historic buildings 'is part of the battle for the sane use of all our resources'.[22] The Mentmore sale in 1977, in which Government refused to intervene, fanned the coals which were to burst into the flaming heritage industry in the next decade.

More immediately, the Mentmore sale provoked the House of Commons' Expenditure Committee's Environment Sub-Committee to hold an inquiry into Dalton's Land Fund which had fallen into disuse since its establishment. This resulted, due to the efforts of SAVE and the other national amenity societies, in the Land Fund's resurrection as the National Heritage Memorial Fund, which was established with independent trustees instead of being part of the Exchequer as the Land Fund had been. The NHMF's budget was never large, but it is ironic, given Dalton's aspirations, that its portfolio of projects was dominated by fine art acquisitions and private estates. When it was in turn reinvented as the Heritage Lottery Fund in 1993, this changed again, and it is arguable that it is now, as described below, much closer to Dalton's vision.

The eighties were a bizarre time for the historic environment, witnessing the birth of the notorious, and vigorous, heritage industry, epitomised by John Mortimer's televised version of *Brideshead Revisited* – Waugh's elegy filmed at Castle Howard in misty golds and sepias, turned into a triumphant advertisement. Could even Mortimer have guessed how it would be received? The Tories under Mrs Thatcher responded to what was clearly a vote-winner – even against their better instincts. The modernist hostility to 'those roving bands of mansion-fanciers and peerage buffs, who go around invading stately homes... for fun and profit in the guise of historical scholarship'[23] was marginalised and increasingly frustrated by the booming heritage industry.

In the nineties, in the wake of the Rio summit, environmentalism overtook heritage conservation in the public imagination, and media attention switched from the saving of country houses to the defence of hillsides and water-meadows. The National Trust's last traditional country house acquisition was Chastleton in 1991. The Heritage Lottery Fund's huge grant to Stoneleigh Abbey in 1998, which attracted widespread media criticism, may be the last of its line. In this context, the rise of the country house to dominate historic conservation can be viewed as a late and aberrant development. Certainly in the light of modern environmentalism and the idea of sustainability, its agenda has looked increasingly narrow.

So we arrive in the present, the public hung-over from the Brideshead champagne, and what we now have is polarity: on the one hand an impatience with the past – but one not tempered by an optimistic sense of progress and governmental stewardship – and on the other institutionalised preservation for its own sake, the result of listing having fallen so far behind reconstruction that it inevitably developed as emergency opposition rather than part of a strategic approach.[24] We can also see, in comments on the Countryside Alliance for example, an alarming echo of the morally charged contempt for country houses now focusing on the countryside as a whole, it being similarly seen by an urban intelligensia as a bastion of privilege.[25]

This is a dangerous moment in the history of conservation, made all the more dangerous by the risk of complacency given what is now the comparative strength of our preservationist legislation for sites and monuments. The despair which fuelled historic conservation in the sixties and seventies, has been diluted as government and developers have responded – by and large – by giving up assaults on such sites as are listed, scheduled, registered. But now the battle has been transferred to the non-registered park, the unlisted building, the site of only local nature conservation value – and here the pressure is worse than ever.

The anti-modern recoil of the last twenty years is often attributed to the accelerating pace of environmental change and the perception that 'we have an unprecedented capacity to change and destroy what has gone before'.[26] But in fact such 'violent and enormous' change was the spur cited by Clough Williams-Ellis in 1928: the rate of change and capacity for destruction are always unprecedented.

I would venture to suggest therefore that it be attributed also to the increasing perception of individual powerlessness (a sense Williams-Ellis certainly did not share), as power is centralised first by government – we must wait and see whether regionalisation is just a smoke-screen – and ultimately by international capital, with its remorseless insistence on maximising returns. A recent survey indicates that of the top ten most powerful people in the United Kingdom, seven are businessmen and only two are elected politicans.[27] These economic forces were largely absent from the England threatened by the Octopus: to us, used if not reconciled to seeing Macdonalds M's at the entrance to every town, Williams-Ellis's questions such as, why do all the petrol pumps have to be painted in such violent colours seem hopelessly naïve.[28] The folk-hero status accorded to the tunnel-digger Swampy in the wake of the A30 and Manchester airport protests is also testimony to the breadth of popular disquiet at centralised, undemocratic decision-making.

However it is interesting, heartening even, to see the recent disappearance of the word Nimby – a crass disparagement of grass-roots action, coined, or at least used with relish, by Nicholas Ridley – and a return at least to the rhetoric of community, the civic realm and public responsibility.

We can see this clearly in the report of the Urban Taskforce 1999, but most dramatically in the Heritage Lottery Fund's Urban Parks Programme. Given that until it was made a lottery distributor the NHMF was frankly elitist, the Urban Parks Programme represents the most astonishing initiative. Lord Rothschild as champion of run-down inner-city playgrounds is not a headline anyone in 1995 could have foreseen. But we have witnessed history in the making with the UPP. It has profound implications for what we define as heritage and, one would hope, for the future of conservation.

The most pioneering aspect of the UPP, and one which is now under pressure as demand outstrips even the HLF's resources, was that it offered grants without reference to national definitions of what constituted heritage merit. Instead of assessing sites on the basis of the *Register*, it gave the initiative to the applicant, to demonstrate a site's historic interest. This meant that sites of 'only' local historic interest were recognised as being as important *in terms of public benefit* as those of national historic interest. The knock-on effect has been to revolutionise local authorities' view of their historic environment, with local lists or local 'heritage audits' now being compiled by many of the more enlightened, often with the help of local amenity societies such as county gardens trusts.

This linkage of *public benefit* to *heritage benefit* in the HLF's criteria, has been augmented by the Secretary of State's 1997 Directions to the lottery distributors which includes requirements that grants should address access, the needs of young people and social deprivation. If this seems incongruous in relation to the country house, it seems perfectly suited to the urban park, and should remind us of Octavia Hill and William Morris's belief that conservation and social justice were united causes. The HLF has deprecated any role in policy-making, because English Heritage is the lead body in the sector, but of course every decision on giving or not giving a grant is establishing implicit policy. Guided by those Directions, the HLF has had an important, if not always deliberate, influence in establishing a more democratic concept of heritage.

In the heritage establishment there is still resistance towards urban parks. And yet the urban park and the Urban Parks Programme are hugely popular and widely supported politically – in November 1999 the arts minister stated that 'the Government certainly recognises the extraordinary importance of parks';[29] ministers were apparently arguing over who got to make the first announcement of the UPP. A MORI poll for the HLF revealed it was far and away the most popular of HLF projects. At the same time, mainstream heritage remains in a ghetto politically. The unease with which aristocratic heritage was viewed earlier in the century has survived the seventies and eighties, with both the Major and Blair governments reluctant to act over VAT, and cutting funding to the NHMF and to English Heritage. Unfortunately for the rest of the historic environment, conservation's marriage to the country house has cost it dear in terms of political and public support: Chris Smith mentioned heritage only three times in his book on culture, and recently omitted any mention of conserving the historic environment from the objectives of his Department of Culture, Media and Sport;[30] media scrutiny of benefits in lottery grants to the privileged is intense and ready to be extremely critical – witness the furore over Stoneleigh, the Churchill papers, or the Royal Opera House.

Mainstream heritage could learn from the urban parks experience. The emphasis it put on public benefit, the importance of access, the inclusion of new buildings or features designed to regenerate a park, rather than just its repair, and the case for heritage merit being handed to local authorities to make, rather than reserved for a central ivory tower, have all made the UPP popular. SAVE has now divorced the country house and has turned the spotlight on other kinds of historic building – notably hospitals and asylums – and addressed the hard-nosed economic benefits of conservation in terms of development. The National Trust in the nineties has not acquired any more country houses but has instead diversified into a more democratic notion of heritage: the Southwell workhouse, Paul Macartney's early home, Mr Straw's semi-detached house at 7 Blyth Grove, Workshop, the Victorian suburban villa, Sunnycroft, at Wellington near Telford. And of course, its biggest single campaign of the 1990s was to acquire Snowdon, a campaign wholly in line with its original aims.

This brings us back to PPG15 and the whole question of defining heritage: whose 'cultural heritage' and whose 'sense of national identity'. The relevance of that word 'cherished' to new ideas on sustainability will become clear shortly. But it is also important because it cuts straight to the emotional, non-expert response of those who witness such remnants on a day-to-day basis, in the context of everyday life, rather than in the context, for example, of an expert theme study by English Heritage. In 1928, Clough Williams-Ellis wrote that,

> a happy awareness of beauty about us should and could be the everyday condition of us all. 'The beauty about us' – that is, the beauty of country, town and village, the normal visible setting of our ordinary everyday lives – not that which is mewed up in galleries and museums or between the covers of books.[31]

This is bang on, but the problem for us with Williams-Ellis was his undemocratic certainty of what constituted beauty. Conservation from Morris and Ruskin to Williams-Ellis and Marcus Binney has been hampered ironically by its greatest champions' narrow understanding of what merits preservation. Williams-Ellis confessed to feeling that,

> seemly architecture and a gracious landscape are sufficient ends in themselves, self-justified, regardless of their social implications… That view, treating mankind as a mere foreground to inanimate beauty, as just figures in a landscape, cannot, I must own, be intellectually defended. I have to concede that no sensible person is likely to concern himself about visual beauty, its creation or preservation, save with reference to its human values.[32]

But as just described, maybe inadvertently, the HLF has suggested one way out of school-masterish expert-opinion as the sole arbiter of what should be preserved. The other is suggested by English Heritage's, in particular Graham Fairclough's, work on sustainability. The application of 'sustainability' to the historic environment is one which the conservation lobby has been slow to investigate, but English Heritage's 1997 publication *Sustaining the Historic Environment* identified its enormous potential not just for conservation but for giving conservation mainstream status.

Sustaining the Historic Environment begins by questioning the objective nature of valuations of the cultural heritage, as opposed to ecological conservation – our reasons for preserving it are 'less absolute'. The document goes on, 'It is only worth doing if it has high levels of public involvement'. Moreover, a sustainable approach means extending definitions beyond the 'best' sites as identified by experts, in recognition of the 'value of local perception and a recognition of other people's non-expert values' – values note, not opinions. It calls for 'a much more finely tuned characterisation of the whole historic resource'; focusing only on parts of the whole 'removes history from its context'. Non-registered, non-listed, non-scheduled sites and monuments 'often have as much if not greater significance for people's day-to-day lives as the nationally significant', and a centralist perspective is different from but 'not necessarily [of] greater importance' than a local one.[33]

This is ground-breaking stuff, and the interesting question is why it has not been taken up more enthusiastically by English Heritage. It must partly be a question of resources – in prioritising its workload, perhaps it is inevitable that the best sites from its perspective get the attention; it still declines to involve itself even in sixty per cent of registered gardens (i.e. the Grade IIs). But it is also a question of culture: to what extent has English Heritage succeeded in, or even approached, reviewing those priorities, and its links to local perspectives? Perhaps regionalisation will help it to become more receptive to 'local values', and alter its top-down perspective. However, when it comes to real policy, that is in its decisions about its grants – and English Heritage faces real cuts of eighteen per cent or seventeen million pounds over the next three years – there may still be a real schism. On the one hand, English Heritage's head of planning has said, 'too little protection [is] given to restoring local environments outside listed buildings and conservation area designations. It is not tenable to limit our concern to design in these areas and consign the rest to the law of the jungle'.[34] On the other, in annoucing a forty million pound scheme to help repair Grade I and II* buildings, which William Filmer-Sankey then of the Victorian Society called 'dosh for toffs', Sir Jocelyn Stevens expounded the classic top-down view, saying that it was 'unarguably best to start where the need is greatest and the heritage value is highest'.[35]

One of the dangers of the top-down perspective, skewed and dominated by lists and schedules, is that it fails to recognise the rich, and wild, mixture of what people consider valuable and worth preserving. And my argument is that the heterogeneity of heritage needs to be acknowledged for its own benefit, for its political benefit and for its public benefit. It has always been the case that what gets conserved is what those with power and influence want to see conserved, but this results in feeble growth. Far better to seek to extend preservation outwards, broaden its base (to switch metaphors) and make it the mass movement it surely can be. Local lists, local gardens trusts, support for allotment holders and for friends of public parks and cemeteries, alliances with Friends of the Earth and other environmental groups, for schools projects, for access. Indeed, so long as it is believed that the principal value in historic sites is outside, removed from, the local environment, they and their conservation will remain politically marginal.

We also need to redress the adversarial nature of conservation in relation to development. Patrick Wright has pointed out that in recent decades 'a partial and backward-looking conception of heritage has been squared off against modernisation in a manner that has constrained our ability to imagine a future'.[36] The adversarial stance we have had to adopt has led conservation dangerously close to disrepute (there is for example gathering pressure on government to re-write the excellent PPG15). But if we can, belatedly, take a creative approach to sustainability that concept gives us the platform to restore our reputation. *The Thames Landscape Strategy*, on which the Garden History Society was very proud to work, has pioneered a fourfold approach to development based on a full understanding of history, ecology the landscape today and public opinion, and has been widely praised for demonstrating 'landscape history... developing a strong new role as the foundation for urban design and landscape assessment. Landscape history can be the basis for moving forward, rather than a conservative reaction which keeps us locked in the past'.[37]

More can be done to bring public opinion and local values into decision-making. At present it still generally takes a quite unreasonable degree of efforts by outsiders to make themselves heard. But political enthusiasm for the principles of Local Agenda 21 established at the Rio summit and now being enshrined in local plans throughout the United Kingdom, offers those in power the opportunity to remove some of those barriers and create opportunities for that local perspective to be brought into the decision-making process.

More can be done in interpreting historic landscapes to draw in a wider audience. Those recent National Trust purchases signal a new approach (based perhaps on recognition that the kitchens were often the most interesting part of the stately home visit). And we can see this in gardens in the success of walled garden restorations: the interpretation of Heligan, for example, puts the gardeners rather than the owners centre-stage and has been hugely popular as a result. The fact that many conservationists consider Heligan vulgar is precisely what has been the problem for the conservationist cause.

In conclusion then, anti-modernism is not the camp for conservation even, or rather especially, now. Conservation has remained a politically and socially marginal concern not only because it has failed to recognise that 'high' culture and 'popular' culture are a continuum, and that the very term 'high' epitomises that failure, but also because of its failure to address the future. We have, as Morris recognised, to see the historic as part of the whole environment, and its role in improving the quality of life, in 'imagining the future', rather than merely preserving the past.

REFERENCES

1 PPG15 para 1.1.
2 Michael Foucault, 'Nietzsche, Genealogy, History' in Paul Rabinow, ed., *The Foucault Reader* (Harmondsworth, 1991), p.89.
3 Ken Powell, 'Heritage is a thing of the past', *Sunday Telegraph*, 10 May 1998, p.8.
4 Anthony Bertram, *Design* (Harmondsworth, 1938), p.93.
5 See Andrew Saint, 'How listing happened' in *Preserving the Past,* ed. Michael Hunter (Stroud, 1996), p.121.
6 Peach and Carrington, 1930, quoted in David Matless, *Landscape and Englishness* (London, 1998), p.53.
7 Clough Williams-Ellis, *England and the Octopus* (London, 1928), pp.139; 169.
8 ibid, p.162.
9 Matless, p.59.
10 Bridget Cherry and Nikolaus Pevsner, *London 2: South* (Buildings of England, Harmondsworth, 1983) p.161.
11 C.E.M.Joad, *A Charter for Ramblers* (1934), quoted Matless, p.62; Harry Peach, *Let Us Tidy Up* (1930), quoted Matless, p.68.
12 *England and the Octopus,* p.141.
13 ibid., p.30.
14 'Caring for the Common Place' in *Our Environmental Heritage, Proceedings of the Heritage Lottery Fund Seminar, March 4, 1998* (Heritage Lottery Fund, 1998).
15 *Transactions of the Ancient Monuments Society*, ns II, 1954, p.35.
16 Sir Lionel Earle to First Commissioner of Public Works,12 Jan 1927, quoted Peter Mandler, *The Fall and Rise of the Stately Home* (New Haven and Yale, 1997), p.174.
17 Memorandum, 'Preservation of the Countryside' for the Town and Country Advisory Committee meeting, 12 November 1937, quoted Mandler, op.cit., p.174.
18 *Parliamentary Debates, Commons*, 1936–37, vol.320, 10 Feb. 1937, col.426, quoted in Saint, op.cit., p.118.
19 James Lees-Milne, *Caves of Ice* (London, 1983), p.172, quoted in Robert Hewison, *The Heritage Industry* (London, 1987), p.61.
20 Mandler, op.cit., p.346.
21 ibid. p.347.
22 'The SAVE report', *Architects' Journal*, December 1975.
23 Reyner Banham, 'King Lut's Navy', *New Society*, 12 November 1981, p.284, quoted Hunter op.cit., p.93.
24 Saint, 'How listing happened' in *Hunter*, ed., esp. p.131.
25 Anthony Browne, 'Countryfolk? Ungrateful, subsidised whingers', *Observer*, 26 September 1999.

26 *Sustaining the Historic Environment* (English Heritage, 1997), p.2.
27 *The Guardian*, 27 September 1999.
28 Williams-Ellis op.cit., p.166.
29 *Report of the House of Commons Culture Media and Sport Committee on the Heritage Lottery Fund*, 1998–99, vol.2, p.143.
30 Department of Culture Media and Sport, *A New Cultural Framework*, December 1998.
31 Williams-Ellis, op.cit., p.23.
32 *Britain and the Beast*, ed. Clough Williams-Ellis, London, 1937, p.91.
33 *Sustaining the Historic Environment* (English Heritage, 1997), passim.
34 *Planning*, 17 September 1999, p.6.
35 *Guardian*, 20 September 1999, p.9.
36 *Guardian*, 4 February 1995.
37 Kim Wilkie, 'History with a Future', *Garden History*, 24:1, Summer 1996, pp.162–64.

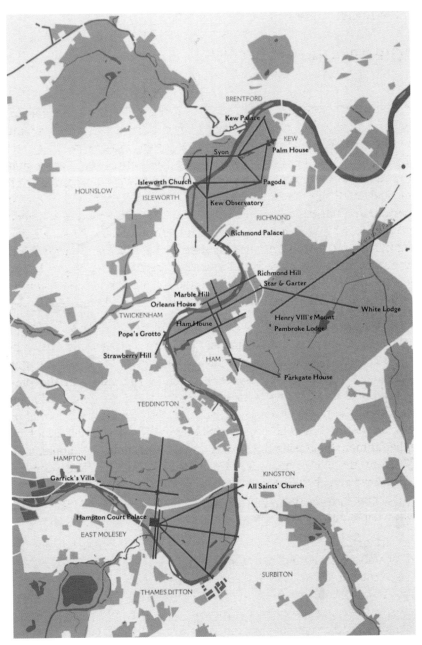

The vista lines which have been created through the centuries to form links between towns, villas and churches along the Thames between Hampton and Kew.

KIM WILKIE

Indignation tomorrow

Indignation is a great source of energy. It seems to be sparked equally by the whiff of a threat to personal territory and by concern for the wider community. The British in particular seem to respond vigorously to a sense of injustice on behalf of the powerless, the vulnerable and the mute – be it mute animals, mute people or mute landscapes. Outrage can stimulate extraordinary gifts of time and intelligent support – as well as money – from those who might otherwise stay silent. Indignation will always play a crucial role in democracy, but in some ways it is quite an inefficient use of energy. It is reactive, confrontational and depends on some injustice being perpetrated in the first place. If the concern and energy for these causes could be harnessed before the outrage were even born and channelled into the planning system to make sure that the direction was right from the start, we would be living in a fine world.

English Heritage is in the midst of reviewing policy for the historic environment as a whole. Consultees are recommending that there should be more democratic access not just to the historic environment itself, but to the way that the historic environment is actually defined and given value. In the previous chapter, David Lambert makes important points about the populist dimensions of heritage. The range of things we value is enormous and the critical part is the *value* not the thing. Losing a grandfather's worthless watch in a burglary can be far more distressing than losing expensive computer equipment. Seeing the tree on the village green felled can seem more tragic than watching the Grade I town hall go up in flames. It is not just that some things can be replaced or rebuilt; it is what the loss represented; what were the memories it could open; what emotions were stirred by merely touching or smelling it?

The work of Common Ground has done much to reveal these values.[1] Quietly and steadily, Sue Clifford and Angela King have been showing what places mean to the people who live in them. They have uncovered the stories hidden in street and field names; the sense of village pride in the variety of apple tree bred over the centuries for that particular soil and climate; and the power of local ballads and ceremonies to connect people and place. In the public consultation at the start of any project it is amazing how the simple act of bringing out historic maps or photographs can trigger huge interest. Seeing what our everyday surroundings looked like a hundred, or even ten years ago seems to hold almost universal fascination. There is an immediate sense of time – charted through shared and personal memories – and a realisation that a place continues to live and change alongside its inhabitants. A place is not just a backdrop for events; it is caught up in the process.

Along with the excitement of change, there is anxiety. We are constantly being told that we are living in a time of great change; that computer and bio-engineering technologies mean that nothing will ever be the same again. Perhaps steam power and railways actually had more impact on the lives of our ancestors than dot.com on ours, but it is the perception of change which counts. The more we feel that everything is in flux, the more we crave some sense of continuity; some fixed points in the flow. Travel and exploration are much easier if there is the security of a home to return to. It is not just the elderly who reach out for continuity. Cutting edge computer game firms choose to make their offices in restored Victorian mills in Manchester and the magic of Harry Potter, with its appeal to children around the world, is set in gothic and suburban England.[2]

So how can these emotions and associations fit into the prosaic English planning system? The Thames Landscape Strategy (Hampton to Kew) was an attempt to understand the ideas which make people feel strongly about the river and to gather the concepts and images into an agreement for how the place should continue to change in the future.[3] The Strategy was based on three years of consultation with local groups, planning authorities and central government agencies. The project combined a study of the local history and nature conservation with an assessment of the current landscape and its contemporary use. Over 200 groups were actively involved in the study, contributing ideas, information and a passion for the place. Members of local and central government as well as amenity societies gave very generous amounts of time and energy to the study. Policies and projects for the river landscape were raised and discussed by all those involved. It was a strategy which drew together the local knowledge and enthusiasm to agree a common way forward. The landscape which had inspired the indignation meetings when the riverside was threatened in 1900 is still able to raise the local interest and energy to come up with a vision for its future a century later. This time though, the energy is raised by optimism for the future rather than by any single threat or outrage.

It is interesting to note how the Strategy began. Rather than as a big idea conceived by government, the Strategy emerged as a small part of the 1991 Thames Connections exhibition which set out to draw attention to the value and plight of the river in London. Most of the exhibitors were building architects, but a small part of the exhibition was set aside for a landscape architect. The landscape exhibit showed how the historic vistas and sightlines along this part of the Thames had determined the layout of the towns, parks and open space in the area. The exhibit showed not only how these views could be restored, but also how they could inspire new vistas and connections. The exhibit happened to catch the eye of some riverside residents, captured the local imagination and grew from there.

One of the key things about place is time. The layers of lives lived and remembered turn location into place. It took time to create; it takes time to understand; and policies for the management and continuing evolution of a place deserve a sensible span of time to take effect. The Thames Landscape Strategy has drawn up policies and projects for the next hundred years. A century is a round cultural concept. It is the period it takes native trees to reach maturity. And it is a time span which allows for buildings to reach the end of their economic life and for past mistakes to be demolished and replaced by more imaginative developments. It also puts the city and the landscape in a proper perspective – places which look through generations, elections and environmental change. The linking of long-term policies and immediate projects in one thought process and document has the advantage of a broad guiding vision relating directly to things happening on the ground.

With such ambitious aims and so many different groups to embrace, a co-ordinator for the Strategy has been essential. Donna Clack has steered the project through its first six years. She has managed to keep national agencies, local authorities and local amenity societies involved and feeling as though the Strategy is alive, relevant and responding to their needs. She has also succeeded in raising funds for the project, so that over 60 per cent of the support comes from private sources. There is a new interest in the river and its future – a sense that it belongs to the local people and that their voice can actually make a difference to the way that it is managed and developed. There is inevitably frustration that some projects are not happening fast enough. There are conflicts between the desire for development and the need to conserve open space. There is friction between those who would like to see historic landscape features restored and those who would prefer a new urban wilderness. But the main thing is that people are looking hard at their surroundings, arguing about them and feeling involved in their future. The value of the place has been acknowledged and the understanding of the character has been explored. Local people are participating in the planning process and central government is responding by calling in controversial schemes for adjudication.

Inspired by the agreements on the Thames from Hampton to Kew, local amenity societies on the next eighteen kilometres downstream, Kew to Chelsea, have banded together as the West London River Group to persuade government to fund a similar study for their part of the Thames. The economic boom and the pressure for riverside development has led to much discussion about how London should evolve around its river. The sites of redundant waterworks, gasworks and playing fields are targeted as brownfield sites ripe for urban renewal. However these areas of open land are also part of the rhythm of waterfront towns and intervening green space which characterise the form of the landscape and communities through the West London Thames. A Thames Strategy should be able to integrate these issues into a fuller context, crossing local authority boundaries and local interests, and reaching some consensus ahead of site by site indignation – before the bulldozers move in, the trees come down and the indignation erupts.

The Thames Landscape Strategy has sometimes been dismissed as a one-off – a plan for an Arcadian idyll of international significance. What about the less glamorous landscapes and the inner city? Does this approach have any relevance for them? The south bank of the Thames in Southwark around London Bridge is as gritty and inner urban as Richmond and Kew are pastoral and suburban. The English Heritage study for the Borough at London Bridge has however succeeded on similar principles to the Thames Landscape Strategy.[4] The extent and time span of the study has been less ambitious, but the approach of involving the local people, understanding the character of the area and agreeing a long term plan based on the public spaces and movement has been accepted.

The Borough at London Bridge is one of the oldest areas of London. There are some fine buildings, such as Southwark Cathedral, but the real magic of the area lies in its rough, utilitarian history as the victualling, entertainment and red light district of the capital, safely across the water from the financial propriety of the City. The ancient market and cathedral still lie at the heart of the area, supported by a beleaguered but long-established community. Impressions of the place hover between images of Blade Runner filmsets and Chaucer's inns, Shakespeare's Globe and Dickens's prison. Areas of dereliction and much-loved Victorian public housing sit beside new developments such as Vinopolis and the Bankside power station, transformed into Tate Modern. Proposals for the Greater London Authority building, the largest teaching hospital in Europe, a new Thameslink rail viaduct and the much-needed improvement of London Bridge Station will accelerate radical change.

Southwark Borough Council, anxious to bring regeneration to the deprived area, has shunned grand masterplans which could slow and hamper investment. Now suddenly, after more than twenty years of inactivity, development is scrambling into the area. The question has been how to guide regeneration to respond to the special character of the Borough. Uncontrolled development of glass and chrome blocks, typical of any other booming city around the world, could disinfect the place of its particular identity and leave the area bland and out-of-date in a decade or so. Regeneration needs to last and the special character of a place – in its community and stories as well as its physical fabric – can keep an area alive and attractive beyond the first burst of investment.

The shape and character of the Borough at London Bridge have been determined by trade, movement and improvisation. It is still a place of movement, located at one of the main commuter cross-roads and public transport interchanges in the capital. Following an intense period of consultation with key players – from the cathedral and the market to the local community groups and central government – it was agreed that the area should be planned around its public spaces and the flow of movement between them. The brief for individual buildings can be set in relation to the spaces they help to form. This is not a grand masterplan, but it does give a coherence to the city from the point of view of those who use it. The public are still able to influence their realm and the process of involvement is locked into the system. The proposed rail viaduct in particular is stimulating much indignation. This kind of targeted vigilance will always have a critical role. There is however the possibility for the integration of local feeling, concern and pride into the planning of the place so that future developments can fit a pattern which has broad agreement.

So how do you tap the energy of indignation early enough to prevent outrage? Who do you consult and how? Many methods of community consultation have evolved. 'Planning for real' techniques can be useful for drawing in a broad range of the public off the street to plot what should happen to their patch in a direct and visual way. At the other end of the spectrum, focus groups can concentrate detailed discussions on particular issues. The internet also opens possibilities for new kinds of consultation and interaction. Each technique has its strengths and ability to reach another section of the people whose environment is being affected, but there is no substitute for just going to talk to people.

Consultation takes time and skill if it is really to reach and reflect what the community is thinking. It is also expensive. The method used for the Thames Landscape Strategy and the Borough at London Bridge studies has been to talk to the key players first and then consult more and more widely as each person recommends several others for consultation. Key players include community leaders, amenity societies, central government agencies, key landowners, key investors and local authority members and officers. Each person or body has a slightly different understanding of the situation and different priorities for the future.

The important thing for the consultant is to go to see each representative individually before any big meetings are arranged. Discussions should be wide-ranging and explore the special character of the place, regardless of what plans may be afoot. The memories and associations – good and bad – between the person and the place need to be understood before going on to discuss what should happen next. The complexity of the sense of place will gradually emerge. Often descriptions of the character will be fairly similar, although reactions to that character can be diametrically opposed. This kind of personal interview is the best way to get to know a place and to understand what it evokes in the people who live and work there. It also gets people thinking and involved before any kind of report is produced or any proposals are put forward. Springing fully formed plans on a community destroys their sense of belonging and being a part of the continuing evolution of a place.

Historical research can also reveal a great deal. Maps and paintings show how an area has evolved. Written descriptions can give a good insight into how people have reacted to the place before and how current impressions have been formed. Gradually a sense of the place will emerge and it will probably change and deepen the more people are consulted and take time to look and consider what they think. One meeting is not enough. It is important to go back after the first exploration to talk about reactions from other people and to start forming suggestions for the way forward. When one finally starts to reach conclusions, any report should be circulated in draft and comments absorbed or acknowledged. The final document should then come as no surprise and simply act as the confirmation of the long series of discussions. It should also leave room for evolution as the place continues to change.

This kind of consultation relies on someone who has the time to visit all the key players and gradually combine and inform the results of the discussions. Interviews need to be sufficiently intimate and personal to pick up all the nuances of the place. The process is not formulaic and the work cannot be sub-contracted to lots of different people to save time. Each consultation informs the next and each issue tends to cross over into others. At London Bridge, for example, concerns over servicing Borough Market relate to the functioning of the cathedral, traffic flows over London Bridge, pedestrian flows from the station, noise levels in surrounding housing, council paving policies and so on and so on. All the ideas need to coalesce in one coherent series of discussions, leading to imaginative and locally focused proposals.

This sort of approach is perhaps a little too free-form for the traditional statutory system. It is however well suited to Supplementary Planning Guidance. The Thames Landscape Strategy could never have happened as a standard part of the statutory process, without being adopted as SPG first. It needed the freedom of standing aside from the system to come up with new ideas and approaches. Without the further filter of being incorporated into the statutory apparatus through Unitary Development Plan Reviews, local authorities could never have been as relaxed in considering fresh policies. Turning contentious cross-borough policies straight into the legislation would have been impossible. The *ad hoc* nature of this kind of consultation would also not have been acceptable without the secondary layer of full statutory consultation at a later stage. As it was though, discussion was able to range freely through government bodies and amenity societies without the fear that some irrevocable policy issue was at stake. By the time it came to formulating the final policy wordings, thinking had advanced to a stage where much more imaginative consensus was possible.

Indignation is one of the great safety checks provided by democracy. The Thames Landscape Strategy and Borough at London Bridge studies manage to incorporate many of the ideas and passions into an agreement before they erupt in indignation, but it is not always possible. The very nature of these studies makes it hard to set down a template for the future. People and places being what they are, it is probably unwise to attempt a 'how-to' solution. Perhaps the closest one can get is to set down three main principles which might help:

1 UNDERSTANDING OF PLACE

Place is the merging of lives into land. The way a town or house or corner of land is remembered; the ideas and emotions it stimulates; the identities and associations it carries – these are what make place. The personal and passionate nature of these associations fuel the energy of indignation. The most essential part of understanding place is learning how to listen and really being interested in what you hear. Anecdotal stories will often carry as much significance as archaeological evidence in local minds. The trick is to discover where the stories overlap and where there is agreement on what gives the place its character. The local rookery may have more bearing on the perceived character than the particular style of Georgian sash windows. That is not to say that one has intrinsically more importance than the other, just that the rooks may impinge more consciously and directly on the lives of the inhabitants. Historical research, nature conservation assessment and the pattern of contemporary life will all contribute to the picture. The eighteenth-century concept of the animated prospect is still completely relevant. It is not just the scene one has to grasp – it is the life and movement which animate it. The public spaces and the way people move between them is the key to urban design.

2 UNDERSTANDING OF CHANGE

The social and economic factors which continue to shape and change place need to be equally understood. How people live and where they are employed continue to be integral to the process. The forces of change can only be guided if the forces themselves are properly understood. Decisions about what to keep and what to replace have to be made in the context of what comes next. Priorities for conservation need to be set on a national and international level as well as on the basis of local distinctiveness. It is the same with nature conservation as with architectural history. Sites of Special Scientific Interest are weighed against the setting of Grade I listed buildings and against regional employment and transport targets. If the need for change is fairly argued and the impact on the local identity and place fully understood, it may be possible to side-step the no-change:sweep-it-all-away tug of war. The discussion could shift into the realm of how the change can best be accommodated in the cherished and complicated pattern we carry with us.

The final principle is to do with the management of place. Over the past few decades 'preservation' has been replaced by 'conservation' as an acceptable term for saving for the future. More recently 'stewardship' has emerged as an even more appropriate concept. Stewardship manages to convey the idea of caring for our surroundings to enable them to survive for succeeding generations. Stewardship can apply to land and water as well as to buildings and communities. Agreement needs to be reached not only on what to take forward but also how to do it. Place is not static; it continues to change. Agreement on stewardship may be the way to smooth the process of change while respecting the resonance of place. If this can find a place in a more responsive planning system it may be the channel for the energy of indignation in the future.

Ruskin understood that a sense of continuity does not have to stop new ideas – just the opposite. The deeper the root, the greater the range of nutrients. When it comes to regenerating cities, the history and character of a place can make a big difference to the long term appeal. Redevelopments which are inspired by the identity of an area can capture a uniqueness which draws people long after the fizz of new buildings has passed. The polished granite and glass of eighties and nineties developments have a bland sameness throughout the world – a lack of personality – which limit their commercial attraction. They go out of fashion. Whereas the cities which have regenerated with some special flair or eccentricity stand out as places where people continue to choose to visit or invest. The canal areas of Manchester and Leeds have managed to stimulate new development which is fresh and original and links straight into the character and stories of each place.

This then is the way forward for the heritage bodies. The conservation of national treasures is clear and relatively uncontroversial. The understanding and perpetuation of local character – though it was clear enough to Morris – is newer territory. It is complicated and time consuming to uncover local identity and work with people's memories and ideas. Ultimately though, this is where heritage lies. In the minds and customs of those who are alive today.

The concept, so well understood by the pioneers of conservation, but which now seems to elude the word 'heritage', is a sense of place, a respect for memory and an ease with the long history of forms and flows which can make design resonate. We need to revive a thought process which loves to understand how we got here and uses it as a springboard for the next inspiration.

REFERENCES

1   Angela King and Sue Clifford, *Holding your Ground: An Action Guide to Local Conservation* (Maurice Temple Smith Ltd, 1985).

2   J.K.Rowling, *Harry Potter and the Sorcerer's Stone* (Arthur A. Levine Books, 1998).

3   Kim Wilkie, *The Thames Landscape Strategy – Hampton to Kew* (Thames Landscape Steering Group, 1994).

4   English Heritage, *The Borough at London Bridge – An Urban Study* (English Heritage, November 1999).

Key events in the amenity movement

1865   Commons and Footpaths Preservation Society (CFPS) founded

1870s   Epping Forest and Hampstead Heath campaigning

1875   Cockburn Association founded

1876   Kyrle Society founded by Miranda and Octavia Hill

1877   The Society for the Protection of Ancient Buildings (SPAB) founded by William Morris

1882   Ancient Monuments Protection Act

1882   Metropolitan Public Gardens Association (MPGA) founded

1886   Selborne Society founded

1889   Royal Society for the Protection of Birds (RSPB) founded

1893   Society for Checking the Abuses of Public Advertising (SCAPA) founded

1895   National Trust founded

1902   Act to save the View from Richmond Hill

1907   National Trust Act

1908   Royal Commission for Historic Monuments (RCHM) founded

1909   Housing and Town Planning Act

1924   Ancient Monuments Society founded

1926   Council for the Preservation of Rural England (CPRE) founded

1931   National Trust for Scotland founded

1932   Town and Country Planning Act. First rural planning

1935   Ramblers' Association founded

1937   National Trust country houses scheme inaugurated

1941   National Monuments Record (NMR) set up

1944   Town and Country Planning Act: Listing of Buildings (extended 1947)

1946   Land Fund set up as war memorial

1949   National Parks and Access to the Countryside Act: Ten parks designated

1949   Nature Conservancy set up. Nature Reserves and Sites of Special Scientific Interest (SSSIS)

1950   Gowers Report on country houses

1953	Historic Buildings and Ancient Monuments Act
1955	First Green Belt established
1957	Civic Trust founded
1958	Victorian Society founded
1965	Garden History Society (GHS) founded
1967	Civic Amenities Act. Conservation Areas
1968	Town and Country Planning Act
1968	Countryside Act established the Countryside Commission
1970	Friends of the Earth founded
1972	Joint Committee of National Amenity Societies set up
1972	Woodland Trust founded
1974	Town and Country Amenities Act
1974	Victoria and Albert Museum exhibition *Destruction of the Country House*
1975	European Architectural Heritage Year
1975	Architectural Heritage Fund
1975	SAVE founded
1979	Thirties Society founded (now Twentieth Century Society)
1980	National Heritage Memorial Act
1983	Common Ground founded
1983	National Heritage Act
1984	English Heritage and Historic Scotland formed, taking over the roles of the Historic Buildings Council and Ancient Monuments boards
1992	Rio Earth Summit
1993	National Lottery Act; major impact on heritage funding
1994	Heritage Lottery Fund
1994	Planning Policy Guidance 15. Major restatement of conservation policy
1997	Thames Landscape Strategy published
2000	Local Heritage Initiative
2000	Department of Culture, Media and Sport Heritage Policy Review

Addresses

Ancient Monuments Society, St Anne's Vestry Hall, London EC4V 5HB (020 7236 3934)

Association of Gardens Trusts, 70 Cowcross Street, London ECIM 6EJ (020 7251 2610)

Cadw, Crown Buildings, Cathays Park, Cardiff CFI 3NQ (01222 500200)

Civic Trust, 17 Carlton House Terrace, London SWIY 5AW (020 7930 0914)

Cockburn Association, Trunks Close, 55 High Street, Edinburgh EHI ISR (0131 557 8686)

Common Ground, PO Box 25309, London NW5 IZA (020 7267 2144)

Council for the Protection of Rural England, Warwick House, 5–27 Buckingham Palace Road, London SWIW OPP (020 7976 6433)

Countryside Agency, John Dower House, Crescent Place, Cheltenham, Glos. GL50 3RA (01242 584270)

Countryside Council for Wales, Plas Penrhos, Ffordd Penrhos, Bangor, Gwynedd LL57 2LQ (01248 370444)

English Heritage, 23 Savile Row, London WIX IAB (020 7973 3000)

English Nature, Northminster House, Peterborough, Cambs. PEI IUA (01733 455000)

Friends of the Earth, 26–28 Underwood Street, London NI 7JQ (020 7490 1555)

Garden History Society, 70 Cowcross Street, London ECIM 6EJ (020 7608 2409)

Georgian Group, 6 Fitzroy Square, London WIP 6DX (020 7387 1720)

Heritage Lottery Fund, 7 Holbein Place, London SWIW 8NR (020 7591 6000)

Historic Scotland, Longmore House, Salisbury Place, Edinburgh EH9 ISH (0131 668 8705)

Joint Committee of National Amenity Societies, St Anne's Vestry Hall, London EC4V 5HB (020 7236 3934)

Metropolitan Public Gardens Association, 3 Mayfield Road, Thornton Heath, Croydon, Surrey CR7 6DN (020 8689 4197)

National Trust, 36 Queen Anne's Gate, London SW1H 9AS (020 7222 9251)

National Trust for Scotland, 28 Charlotte Square, Edinburgh EH2 4ET (0131 243 9300)

Open Spaces Society, 25a Bell Street, Henley-on-Thames, Oxon. RG9 2BA (01491 573535)

Ramblers' Association, 1–5 Wandsworth Road, London SW8 2XX (020 7582 6878)

Royal Society for Nature Conservation (The Wildlife Trusts), The Green, Witham Park, Waterside South, Lincoln LN5 7JR (01522 544400)

Royal Society for the Protection of Birds, The Lodge, Sandy, Beds. SG19 2DL (01767 680551)

SAVE, 70 Cowcross Street, London EC1M 6BP (020 7253 3500)

Scottish Natural Heritage, 12 Hope Terrace, Edinburgh EH9 2AS (0131 447 4784)

Society for the Protection of Ancient Buildings, 37 Spital Square, London E1 6DY (020 7377 1644)

Thames Landscape Strategy, Holly Lodge, Richmond Park, Richmond, Surrey TW10 5HS (020 8948 3209)

Twentieth Century Society, 70 Cowcross Street, London EC1M 6EJ (020 7250 3857)

Victorian Society, 1 Priory Gardens, London W4 1TT (020 8994 1019)

Woodland Trust, Autumn Park, Dysart Road, Grantham, Lincs. NG31 6LL (01476 581111)

Acknowledgements

The authors and publisher would like to thank Alan Baxter, who has done so much to bring amenity societies together (some even under his own roof), Alan Eliot of the Wimbledon Society, Julian Pooley of the Surrey History Centre, the Librarian of the Civic Trust, Sonia Crutchlow of the William Morris Society and Howard Hull the curator of Brantwood and the Ruskin collection; also the amenity societies mentioned throughout the book for information provided. We are particularly indebted to Kate Tiller, who organised the Ruskin Conference for Oxford University of Continuing Education, and the lecturers who contributed papers to it, Lawrence Goldman, Gillian Darley of SPAB and David Elliston Allen. We are very grateful to the Garden History Society Jubilee Fund for a grant to enable us to distribute library copies of the book to leading amenity societies and organisations. All royalties from sales of the book are to be given to the Jubilee Fund.

ILLUSTRATION SOURCES AND CREDITS

Frontispiece   The view from Richmond Hill. Photograph by Lucilla Phelps.

Page 12   The facsimile jacket for the reprint of Clough Williams-Ellis's *England and the Octopus* published by the CPRE. Copyright the Portmeirion Estate.

Page 28   *The Preserved Amenity*, cartoon by Thomas Derrick published in *Punch* summer supplement, 1937. Copyright Punch Illustrations.

Page 46   Vista lines on the Thames. Illustration by Kim Wilkie.

The Garden History Society

The Society has been established for over thirty years. Its main aims are to promote the study of the history of gardening, landscape gardening and horticulture in all its aspects and to promote the protection and conservation of historic parks, gardens and designed landscapes. For further details and application for membership apply to The Director, 77 Cowcross Street, London ECIM 6EJ.

Note on the authors

MAVIS BATEY was for many years Secretary and latterly President of the Garden History Society and a pioneer in garden conservation. She has been an active member of the Oxfordshire Branch of the CPRE and of the Oxford Civic Society and a member of many landscape advisory committees including English Heritage's Garden Committee. During the Second World War she worked as a codebreaker at Bletchley Park and then taught for Oxford University External Studies. As a historian of landscape and literature she is perhaps best known for her books: *Jane Austen and the English Landscape* was followed last year by *Alexander Pope: The Poet and the Landscape*.

DAVID LAMBERT is the Conservation Officer for the Garden History Society. He has had much experience as an amenity society caseworker and lobbyist and has been closely involved with his local county gardens trust in Avon. He is a member of the Heritage Lottery Fund's Historic Buildings and Land Panel and was adviser to the House of Commons select committee inquiry into town and country parks in 1999. Among his publications are *Public Prospects: Historic Urban Parks under Threat* (1993) and *The Historic Public Parks of Bristol* (2000). He has also written a critique of conservation philosophy in *Four Purbeck Arcadias* (New Arcadian Press, 1998).

KIM WILKIE is a landscape architect and urban designer. He is a member of the Royal Parks Advisory Board, English Heritage's Urban Panel and their Historic Areas and Buildings Advisory Committee, the National Trust's Gardens Advisory Panel and the Heritage Lottery Fund's Urban Parks Programme. The focus of his practice, Kim Wilkie Associates, is on the intimate relation between land, culture and place. The practice combines the restoration of historic landscapes with radical new designs and the regeneration of cities springing from their individual character and identity. Projects range from Chile and North America to the Mediterranean and the Russian Arctic Circle. His work on the Thames Landscape Strategy brought a close association with his fellow authors Mavis Batey and David Lambert.